HOW TO DRAW
COOL
CARS

Artist and author
Steve Capsey
at Maltings Partnership

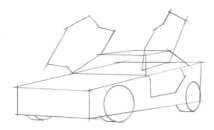
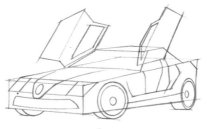
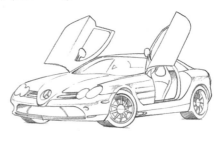

Miles
KeLLY

Contents

Materials

ALL YOU NEED TO START DRAWING CARS IS A PENCIL AND PAPER, BUT YOU CAN COLLECT OTHER MATERIALS AS WELL TO CREATE EXCITING EFFECTS IN YOUR PICTURES.

Felt-tip pens

Using felt-tip pens will give your drawings a cartoonish feel. Use them to define outlines and create dramatic graphics on your cars.

Coloured pencils

Use sharp and blunt pencils for different effects. Press hard on you paper for dark areas and use delicate strokes for highlights in paintwork.

Ruler

When you start to draw cars, a ruler will help you draw the long, straight lines.

Pencils

Soft pencils (marked with a B) make black, smudgy lines that are easy to rub out. Hard pencils (marked H) make light, thin lines.

 Hard pencil

 Soft pencil

Paper

When you start drawing cars, you could use tracing paper to achieve the first stage, or trace different cars for practise. Gridded paper may help you draw the shape of your car.

Different materials

Try experimenting with wax crayons, paints and pastels for different effects. You could even try mixing two different materials together in the same picture.

Basic shapes

TO BEGIN DRAWING CARS YOU NEED TO LEARN HOW TO DRAW STRAIGHT LINES AND BASIC SHAPES, SUCH AS BOXES FOR THE BODY OF A CAR AND ELLIPSES (NARROW CIRCLES) FOR THE WHEELS.

Types of line

Using a ruler will help you draw long straight lines when you start to draw your car. There are different types of lines you can draw with a ruler.

① ——————————————— Keep your pencil steady to produce a straight line.

② ——————————————— By moving your pencil around, you will get a wobbly line.

③ ——————————————— Gently change the angle of your pencil to create slight curves.

④ ——————————————— Use a sharp pencil for a thin line.

⑤ ——————————————— A blunt pencil will form a thick line.

Circles and ellipses

Wheels are round, but they only look like circles when they are viewed straight on. When viewed at an angle they seem thinner and squashed. This shape is called an ellipse.

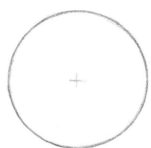

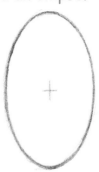

A For a wheel to look like this, you would have to look at the side of a car straight on.

B This is an ellipse. The shape has tight curves at the top and bottom.

C Wheels will look thinner if they are turned at an angle. The more a wheel turns, the thinner it looks.

Rectangles

Practise drawing rectangles of different sizes and angles. They will help you draw your boxes for the body of your car.

Use a ruler to draw a rectangle and try to make your corners tidy.

TRY DRAWING A SHOE BOX. TURN IT AROUND AND DRAW IT FROM DIFFERENT ANGLES. CAN YOU SEE HOW THE SAME BOX LOOKS DIFFERENT?

Box shapes

Boxes will help you draw the basic shape of your car. The boxes below are the same shape, but they look different because they are viewed from different angles.

A This box shape is viewed more from the side, so it looks more in proportion. The front and back of the box look roughly the same size.

B If the same box is viewed more from the front, the front looks much bigger than the back because it is closer to you. This is called perspective.

Three rectangles form the box shape – measure the sides with a ruler to see how they are different lengths at the front and back.

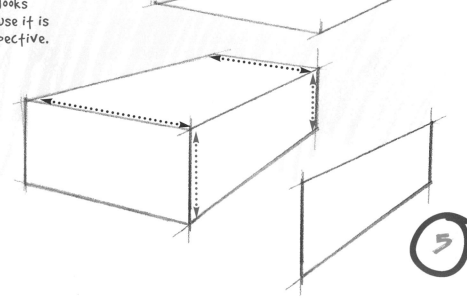

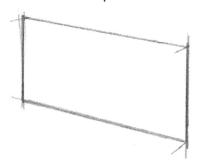

5

Car parts

ONCE YOU HAVE MASTERED DRAWING ELLIPSES AND BOX SHAPES YOU CAN BEGIN TO DRAW YOUR CAR.

Basic car shape

Putting your shapes together will give you the basic shape of your car.

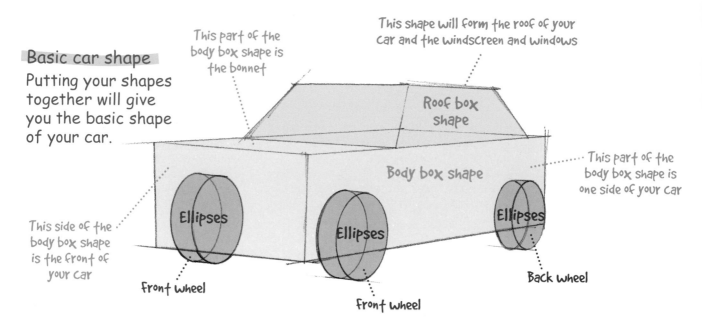

This part of the body box shape is the bonnet

This shape will form the roof of your car and the windscreen and windows

Roof box shape

Body box shape

This part of the body box shape is one side of your car

This side of the body box shape is the front of your car

Ellipses

Ellipses

Ellipses

Front wheel

Front wheel

Back wheel

Car parts

Once you have the basic shape of your car you can begin to add the parts. Many cars have the same parts, even though they may look different.

Windscreen wipers

Windscreen

Roof

Aerial

Windows

Vent

Lights

Radiator grills

Tyre

Number plate

Fog light

Wheel arch

Wheel

Spokes

Wing mirror

Door handle

Drawing wheels

When you start drawing wheels, practise drawing this simplified version.

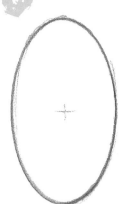
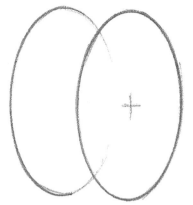
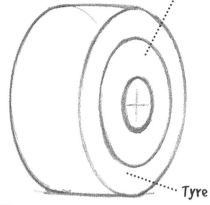

Hubcap

Tyre

(A) Draw an ellipse and mark the centre with a cross.

(B) Draw another ellipse of the same size next to the first one. You don't need to draw the whole thing, as some of the second ellipse will not be visible.

(C) Join the top and bottom edges with a slightly curved line. Add two more ellipses to show the tyre and hubcap.

Complex wheel

When you feel confident drawing simple wheels, you can add details to make your wheels look more complex.

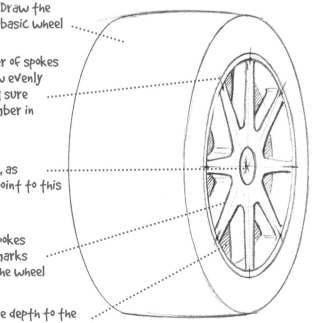

① Draw the basic wheel

② Mark the number of spokes you want to draw evenly around the edge, making sure there are the same number in each half of the wheel

③ Mark the centre, as everything will point to this

④ Draw the spokes from your marks to the centre of the wheel

⑤ Add some depth to the spokes and shading behind to make them stand out

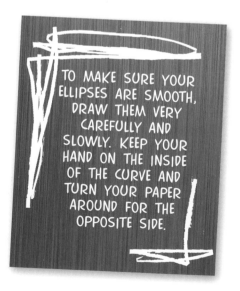

TO MAKE SURE YOUR ELLIPSES ARE SMOOTH, DRAW THEM VERY CAREFULLY AND SLOWLY. KEEP YOUR HAND ON THE INSIDE OF THE CURVE AND TURN YOUR PAPER AROUND FOR THE OPPOSITE SIDE.

Shading

ADDING SHADING TO YOUR CARS WILL MAKE THEM LOOK SOLID AND THREE-DIMENSIONAL.

USE SMALL, CIRCULAR MOVEMENTS WITH A BLUNT PENCIL TO ACHIEVE A SMOOTH SHADE. GRADUALLY BUILD UP YOUR PENCIL MARKS FOR THE DARKER AREAS.

Light and dark

When light shines on your car, the parts nearest the light will be the palest and the parts further away will be darker.

cars are normally lit by the sky above, so the top surfaces will be the palest areas of the car

There is no light shining under the wheel arches, so there will be a lot of shading here

This car is lit from below, so the bottom of the car is the palest and the top surfaces are very dark

Types of shading

There are different ways to shade and they all create different effects.

Stippling
Add lots of dots with a pencil. More dots will make areas look darker.

Hatching
Draw lines the same thickness and the same distance apart.

Cross-hatching
Just like hatching, but add another set of lines crossing at an angle to the first.

Night scene

Drawing cars at night will give you the chance to experiment with shading and different colours.

Use an orange pencil to show where the light falls on your car from streetlights

The light also falls on the ground, so use black and orange pencils to colour it

Use a yellow pencil to show the light coming from the car's headlights

Car lights

Cars have different types of lights and they look different when they are on and off.

Glass lights
Lights are made of glass, so use blue and green pencils to colour them.

Shaped lights
You can draw circles to show the shape of a car's lights through the glass covering.

Lights on
Use yellow and orange colours for lights that are on. The bulb is brightest in the middle, so leave this white.

Texture and colour

ONCE YOU HAVE DRAWN YOUR CAR YOU CAN ADD TEXTURE AND COLOUR. USE DIFFERENT COLOURS AND TECHNIQUES TO CREATE DIFFERENT EFFECTS.

Paint treatments

You can choose what colour you would like your car to be and whether the paintwork will be clean or dirty.

Clean, shiny paint

Using a mixture of dark and light areas to show reflections will make paintwork look shiny.

Dirty, dull paint

There is little contrast between light and dark areas if the paintwork is dirty. Add brown colours for mud splashes.

Tyre tread

You can add tread to your tyres to give them texture. Tyre treads are often a zigzag pattern.

off-road car tyre

The tyres of off-road cars have tread so that they can grip the uneven surfaces.

Racing car tyre

This tyre is completely smooth. The car moves so quickly that the tyres grip the road without needing tread.

ADD HIGHLIGHTS TO DARK COLOURS TO MAKE PAINTWORK LOOK SHINY. YOU CAN LEAVE AREAS OF WHITE PAPER OR USE A WHITE COLOURED PENCIL TO CREATE HIGHLIGHTS.

Reflections

Paintwork that is clean and shiny will show reflections. You can show reflections in paintwork by using different colours.

The roof of the car is slightly blue, as it is reflecting the blue sky

colour some areas darker than others to show reflections

You can see the road reflected in the paintwork of this car

Use a little orange to show the reflection of the ground, or you could use green to show a reflection of grass

Glass

Your car's windscreen, windows and lights are made of glass. Use a blunt pencil to make glass look smooth and colour it using blue and green pencils.

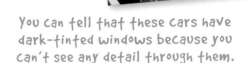

You can tell that these cars have dark-tinted windows because you can't see any detail through them.

The rearview mirrors and steering wheels inside these cars are visible through the glass.

Action

CARS LOOK EXCITING WHEN THEY ARE MOVING. AS WELL AS DRAWING THEM STATIONARY, YOU WILL ALSO WANT TO DRAW THEM IN MOTION.

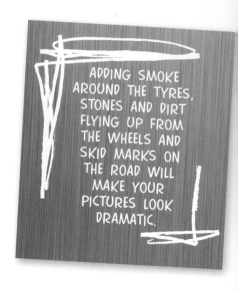

ADDING SMOKE AROUND THE TYRES, STONES AND DIRT FLYING UP FROM THE WHEELS AND SKID MARKS ON THE ROAD WILL MAKE YOUR PICTURES LOOK DRAMATIC.

Racing scene

Try drawing your cars as part of a scene. You could add other cars and a background to your picture.

To give your scene action and a feeling of depth, make distant objects blurred and out of focus

colour and add a pattern to the edge of the racing track

Add smudge lines behind the cars to make them look like they are moving fast

Add tyre marks to the track with black pencil

Draw fluffy white smoke behind the back wheel

Extreme braking

You could draw an action scene in which a car is braking hard on a road.

When drawing smoke, you can add it all the way around a tyre and under the body of the car.

Skid marks on the road can be shown with heavy pencil shading

Add some smoke from the tyres and dust flying up to give a dramatic effect

Draw different sized gaps between the wheels and the wheel arches to show that your car is braking hard

Cornering

When a car goes round a tight corner, the body of the car leans round the bend. This action is called cornering.

You could draw cars cornering on a racing track as part of a scene.

There is only a very small gap between the tyre and the wheel arch

Stones and dirt fly up behind the wheels

The whole body of the car leans as it goes round a tight bend

13

Mini

1 Draw a body box shape. Then draw a roof box shape with sloping sides on top. Add ellipses for the three wheels that will be visible.

The roof box shape does not reach the back

This wheel is further away, so it looks smaller

These wheels are roughly the same size

Draw two ellipses and join the top and bottom edges

2 Define the shape of the car using straight lines. Rub out the sections of the wheels that are hidden behind the body.

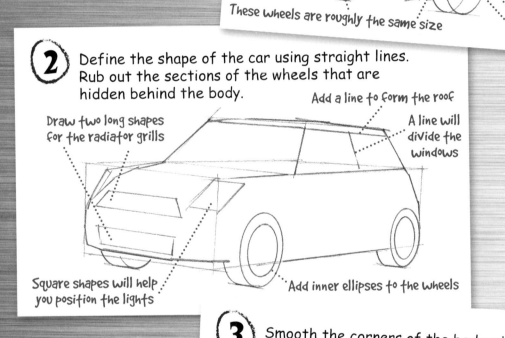

Draw two long shapes for the radiator grills

Add a line to form the roof

A line will divide the windows

Square shapes will help you position the lights

Add inner ellipses to the wheels

3 Smooth the corners of the body with curved lines and start to add extra details.

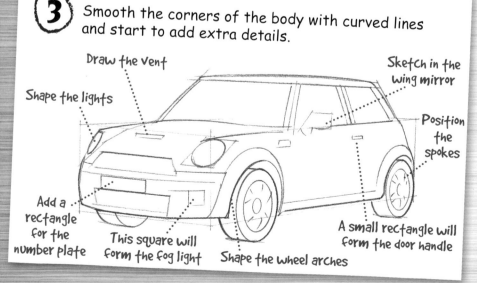

Draw the vent

Sketch in the wing mirror

Shape the lights

Position the spokes

Add a rectangle for the number plate

This square will form the fog light

A small rectangle will form the door handle

Shape the wheel arches

14

4 Erase the guide shapes. Continue adding detail and shape to the features of the car.

Add the aerial ·········

Draw the door and shape the handle

Round off the straight edges and begin to shade the radiator grills

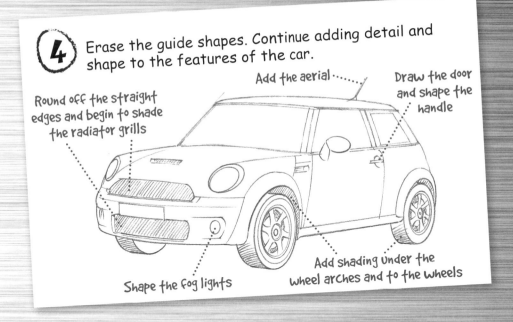

Add shading under the wheel arches and to the wheels

Shape the fog lights

5 Using smooth movements, shade the body of your car with a blue pencil. You can show reflections in the paintwork by colouring some areas darker than others. Leave some white paper showing through for highlights. Use a black pencil for the wheel arches, tyres and radiator grills.

Use a green pencil to show dark ········ areas of glass

Dragster

1 This car has a slightly different body shape to other cars. Draw a long, thin shape getting narrower towards the front for the body. Then add one small box on top and one behind.

This box forms the driver's area

Add the big back wheel – the other is hidden behind the body of the car

Draw two thin front wheels

2 Draw inner ellipses on the wheels. Start to draw the cage, which protects the driver at the back of the car.

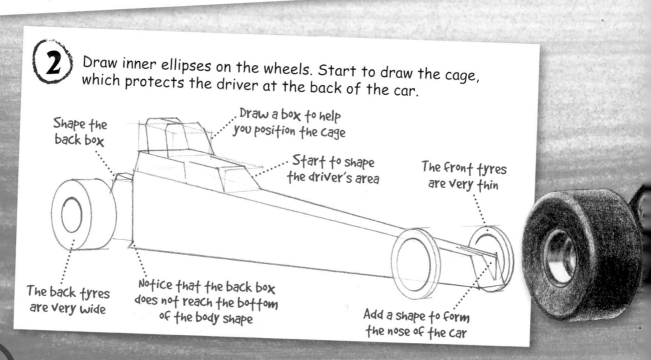

Shape the back box

Draw a box to help you position the cage

Start to shape the driver's area

The front tyres are very thin

The back tyres are very wide

Notice that the back box does not reach the bottom of the body shape

Add a shape to form the nose of the car

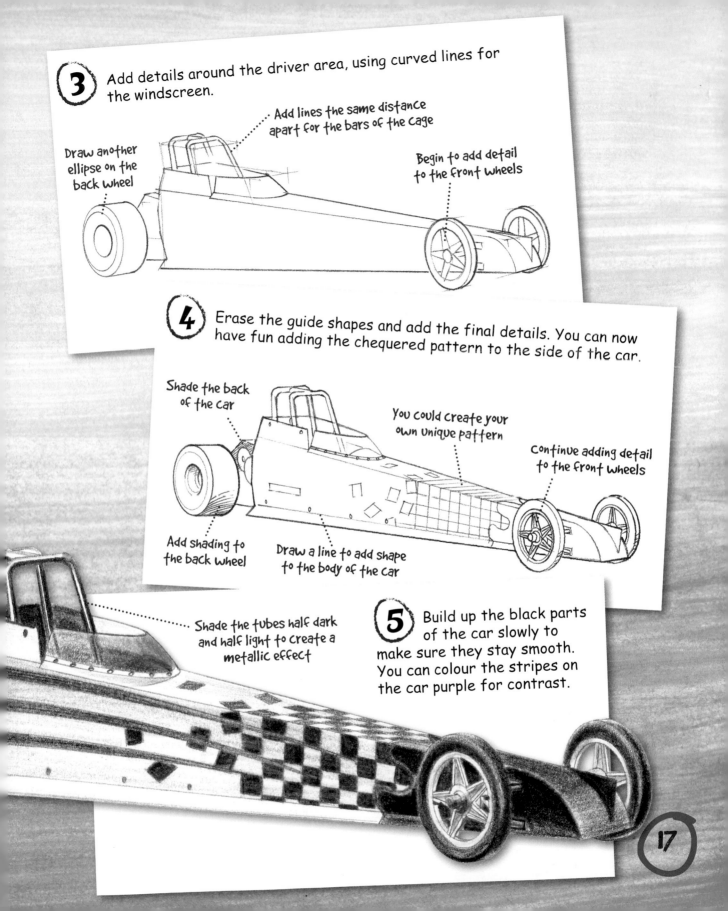

3 Add details around the driver area, using curved lines for the windscreen.

Draw another ellipse on the back wheel

Add lines the same distance apart for the bars of the cage

Begin to add detail to the front wheels

4 Erase the guide shapes and add the final details. You can now have fun adding the chequered pattern to the side of the car.

Shade the back of the car

You could create your own unique pattern

Continue adding detail to the front wheels

Add shading to the back wheel

Draw a line to add shape to the body of the car

Shade the tubes half dark and half light to create a metallic effect

5 Build up the black parts of the car slowly to make sure they stay smooth. You can colour the stripes on the car purple for contrast.

17

4x4

1 Draw a large body box shape for the main part of your car. Add a roof box shape with sloping sides on top.

The topmost part of the roof is barely visible

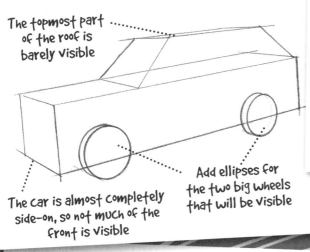

The car is almost completely side-on, so not much of the front is visible

Add ellipses for the two big wheels that will be visible

2 Make the bonnet slope downwards from the windscreen. Add big bumpers to the front and back of the car.

Add another line to complete the roof

Draw a square shape for the lights

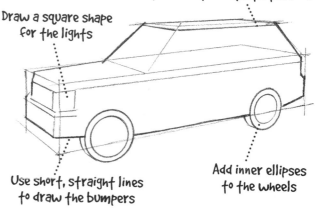

Use short, straight lines to draw the bumpers

Add inner ellipses to the wheels

3 Start to add details to the side of the car, such as the wing mirror and door handles. Add the number plate to the front.

Start to draw the radiator grill with straight lines

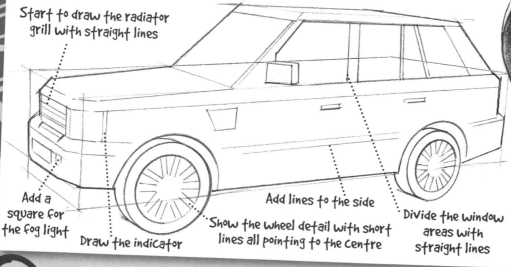

Add a square for the fog light

Draw the indicator

Show the wheel detail with short lines all pointing to the centre

Add lines to the side

Divide the window areas with straight lines

When drawing wheels, the spokes must all be the same size and point towards the centre. If you draw a light circle behind the spokes it will look like the brakes.

4 Rub out the guide shapes. Make all of the corners of the car slightly rounded and continue adding details.

Add the windscreen wipers

There are lots of small circles for the lights

Draw the edges of the doors

Draw indentations behind the door handles

There is a vent on the side of the car

Add shading under the wheel arches

5 The grey paint on the car needs to be very smooth, so take your time and build it up slowly. Colouring the glass half dark and half light will show a reflection. Use an orange pencil to show the indicators.

The wheel arches are very deep and dark, so use a black pencil here

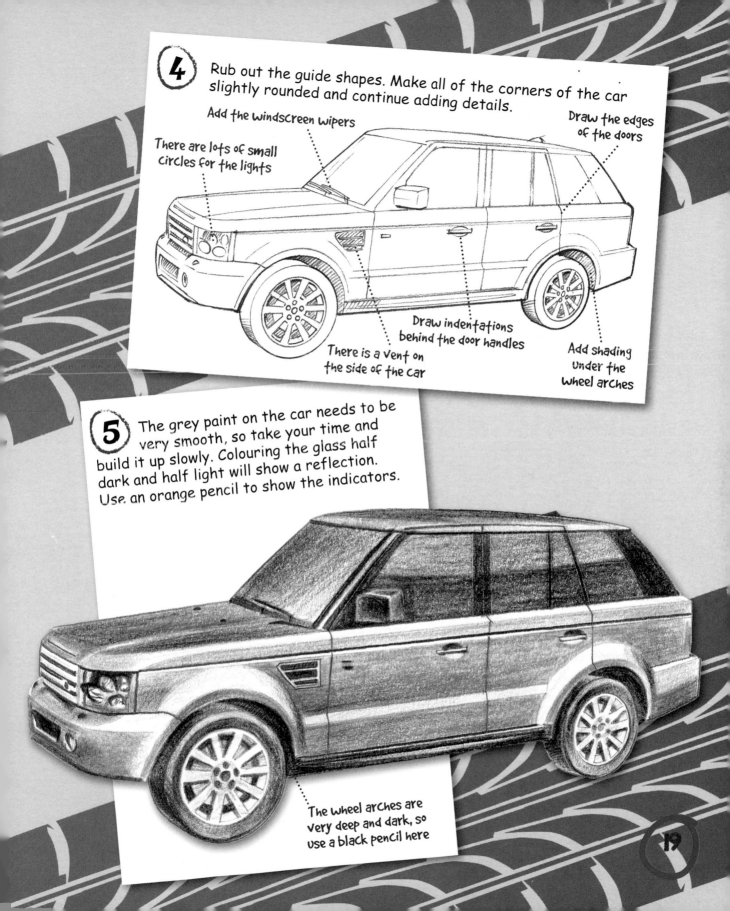

Custom car

1 Draw a large body box shape for the main part of your car. On top of this draw a roof box shape with sloping sides. Add ellipses for the three wheels that will be visible.

The lines at the front of the body box shape are nearly horizontal, as we are viewing the car from the front

To draw flames, start with a yellow pencil and use a soft orange pencil towards the edges. Adding a shadow behind the flames will make them stand out.

Box shapes will become the big wheel arches

2 Start to show the rounded edges of the front and back of the car. Begin to shape the large wheel arches.

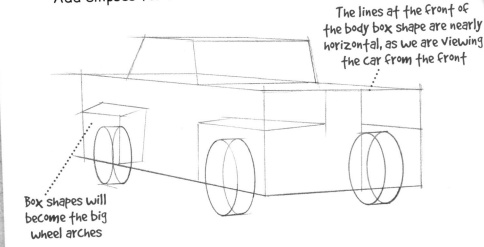

Draw the window shapes with straight lines

Add inner ellipses to the wheels

Use short, straight lines to begin to show the rounded edges

Add the big front bumper

Rub out the sections of the wheels hidden by the body

3 Make all the corners of the car rounded. Using curved lines, add a shape for the large radiator grill to the front, between the lights.

Draw gentle curves over the top of the guidelines to round the wheel arches

Square shapes will help you place the lights

Start to draw spokes in the wheels

4 Erase the guide shapes and draw the final details. You can now add the flame design to the front and sides of the car. Or you could create your own unique pattern.

Draw a small circle for the wing mirror

Use a ruler to draw this long line of trim in sections

Use lines to add detail to the radiator grill

Draw and shade the lights

Soft curves with pointy ends will form the flames

Add shading to the wheels

5 Use lots of reds, oranges and yellows to create the paint design. A hard edge between the flames and the paint will make the flames stand out.

Custom cars have dark glass, so colour it with black and blue pencils

Saloon

Use a blunt pencil and make lots of small, round movements to make glass look smooth. Create the colour with a mixture of blue and green pencils.

1 Draw a sloped body box shape for the main part of the car. Then draw a roof box shape towards the back.

This line slopes upwards slightly

The body box shape slopes down towards the front

The back wheel looks smaller than the front wheel – it is further away

Add the large front wheel

2 Begin to shape the body of your car. Add rough shapes at the front for the lights, radiator grills and number plate.

Draw lines to create the windows

Rough shapes will form the radiator grills

Add inner ellipses to the wheels

3 Use curved lines to shape the corners of the car. Add the wing mirror and two door handles.

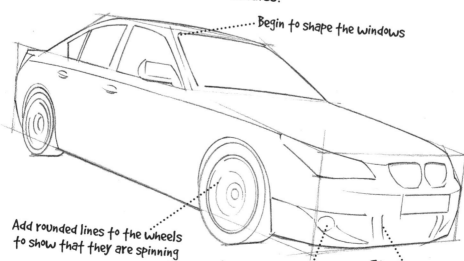

Begin to shape the windows

Add rounded lines to the wheels to show that they are spinning

only one fog light is visible

Start to add detail to the front of your car

22

4 Erase the guide shapes. Draw in the doors and some rough inside detail through the glass.

Draw the passenger head rest

Add a circle for the badge on the bonnet

Start to shade the paintwork to show the shape of the car

Begin to shade the wheels and radiator grills

5 Build up the dark green colour slowly. Leave the surfaces that are angled upwards lighter, as more light falls on them. Use shades of blue to colour the car's lights. You can use gentle fades and sharp edges to show reflections or details through the glass of the windscreen and lights.

The detail in the wheels is blurred because they are spinning

Porsche

1 Draw a large body box shape for the main part of the car and a roof box shape towards the back on top. Add ellipses for the two visible wheels.

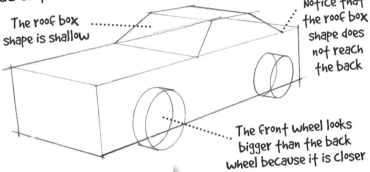

The roof box shape is shallow

Notice that the roof box shape does not reach the back

The front wheel looks bigger than the back wheel because it is closer

2 Start to make the edges rounded using short, straight lines. Draw a pointed shape for the spoiler at the back.

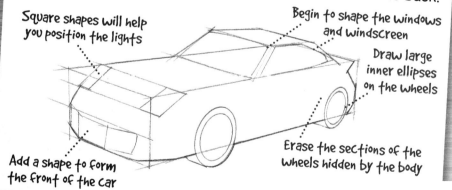

Square shapes will help you position the lights

Begin to shape the windows and windscreen

Draw large inner ellipses on the wheels

Add a shape to form the front of the car

Erase the sections of the wheels hidden by the body

3 Start to make all the corners of the car rounded by drawing smooth curves over the top of the guidelines.

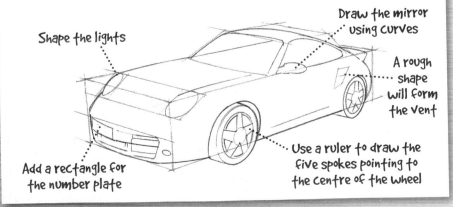

Shape the lights

Draw the mirror using curves

A rough shape will form the vent

Add a rectangle for the number plate

Use a ruler to draw the five spokes pointing to the centre of the wheel

4 Rub out the guide shapes. Draw in the details, making sure they are all smooth and curved.

Add lines of shaping

Draw the door handle and doors

Place the badge

A circle indicates the big brakes behind the wheels

Begin to add shading

The windows are very dark, so use a mixture of black, blue and green

5 Use shades of yellow to colour your car. Adding a little orange and green will make it look even more shiny. Leave some parts white to show where the surface of the car catches the light.

Smart car

1 Draw a sloped body box shape for the main part of the car. Add a roof box shape above it, sloping down to the front of the body box shape.

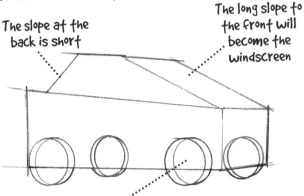

The slope at the back is short

The long slope to the front will become the windscreen

Draw ellipses for the four wheels — they are all visible

2 Start to shape the front and back of the car. Add rough shapes for the seats.

This guideline will be rubbed out because the car's roof is down

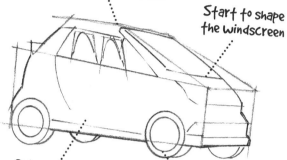

Start to shape the windscreen

Rub out the sections of the wheels you cannot see

Add inner ellipses to the wheels on this side of the car

3 Begin to add detail to the body of the car. Draw nine thin spokes on each of the two visible wheels, all pointing to the centre.

Add the wing mirror

Draw rough shapes for the lights

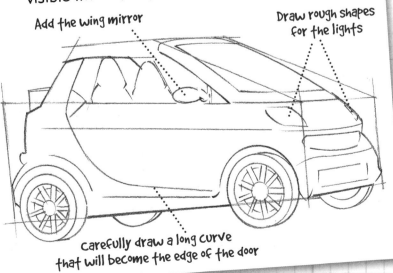

carefully draw a long curve that will become the edge of the door

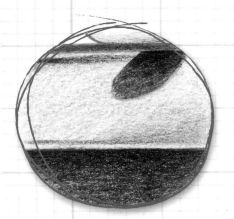

A blunt pencil will help to create a glossy paint effect. Change the level of shading where the panels bend and show shadows with dark shapes.

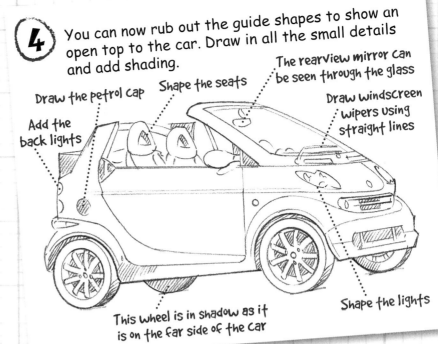

4 You can now rub out the guide shapes to show an open top to the car. Draw in all the small details and add shading.

Draw the petrol cap

Shape the seats

The rearview mirror can be seen through the glass

Draw windscreen wipers using straight lines

Add the back lights

This wheel is in shadow as it is on the far side of the car

Shape the lights

5 This car has a mix of silver and purple panels. Try to build up the colour slowly and make it as even as possible. The paint shows a shadow cast by the wing mirror, so you will need to use a darker purple. Colour the lights at the back of the car red.

Shade lightly above this line, as there is a bend in the body

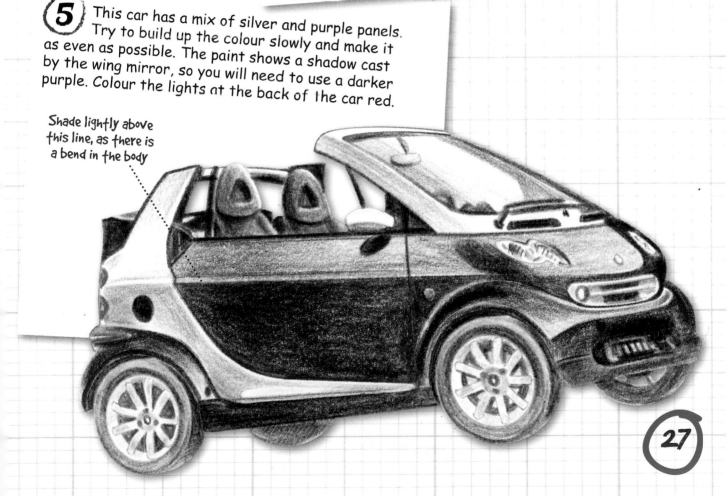

Lamborghini

1 Draw a large body box shape getting slightly lower for the front of the car. Then draw a low roof box shape on top.

This line will help you form the back of the car

The front of the car looks narrow, as we are viewing it from behind

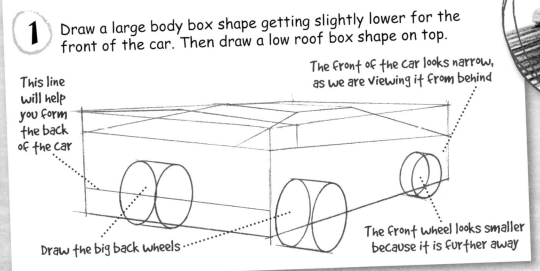

Draw the big back wheels

The front wheel looks smaller because it is further away

Use a sharp pencil for the black rubber skid marks and then use a blunt grey pencil for the smoke. To make the smoke softer, rub it with your finger.

2 Start to shape the body at the back. Add the wheel arches and shape them using straight lines.

Add the large spoiler to the back

Draw a small box shape

Use completely straight lines

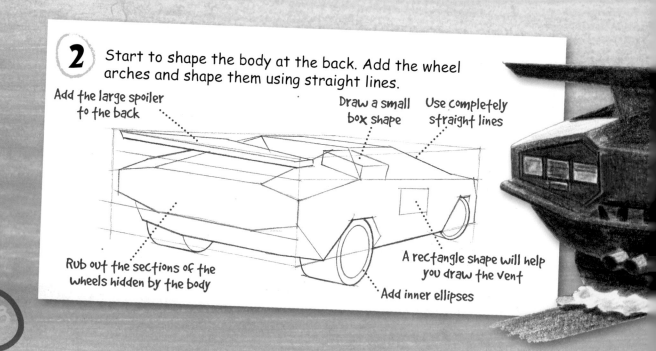

Rub out the sections of the wheels hidden by the body

A rectangle shape will help you draw the vent

Add inner ellipses

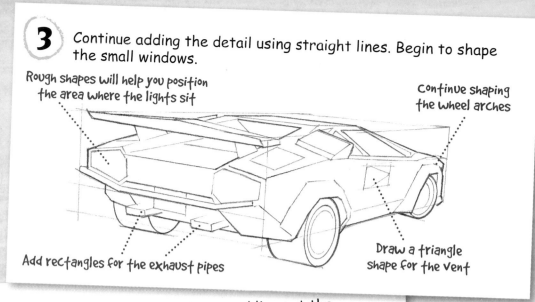

3 Continue adding the detail using straight lines. Begin to shape the small windows.

Rough shapes will help you position the area where the lights sit

Continue shaping the wheel arches

Add rectangles for the exhaust pipes

Draw a triangle shape for the vent

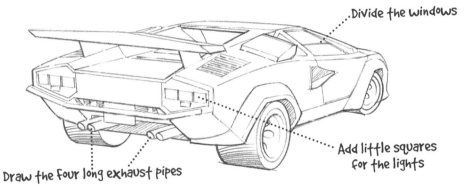

4 Erase the guide shapes. Draw slightly curved lines at the corners of the wheel arches and along the side of the car. Add lots of little details and shading.

Divide the windows

Draw the four long exhaust pipes

Add little squares for the lights

5 Colour the sides of the car with a blunt red pencil. There are lots of hard edges on the car, so the colour will change from dark on the sides to light on the top.

Clouds of white smoke and skid marks under the rear wheels show action and speed

1 Draw a large body box shape that slopes down at the front. Add a roof box shape on top that goes right to the back of the body box shape.

Draw ellipses for the three wheels that will be visible

The box shape is lower on this side — the car is leaning as it goes round a corner

2 Draw lines for the bumper and rectangles for the lights using a ruler. Start to draw the shape of the door.

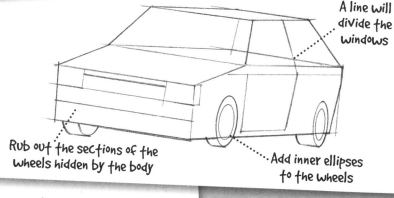

A line will divide the windows

Rub out the sections of the wheels hidden by the body

Add inner ellipses to the wheels

3 Begin to draw the windows and curved wheel arches.

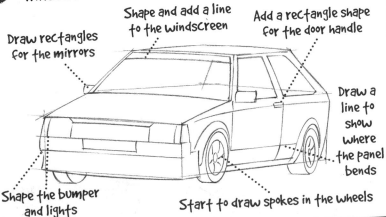

Draw rectangles for the mirrors

Shape and add a line to the windscreen

Add a rectangle shape for the door handle

Draw a line to show where the panel bends

Shape the bumper and lights

Start to draw spokes in the wheels

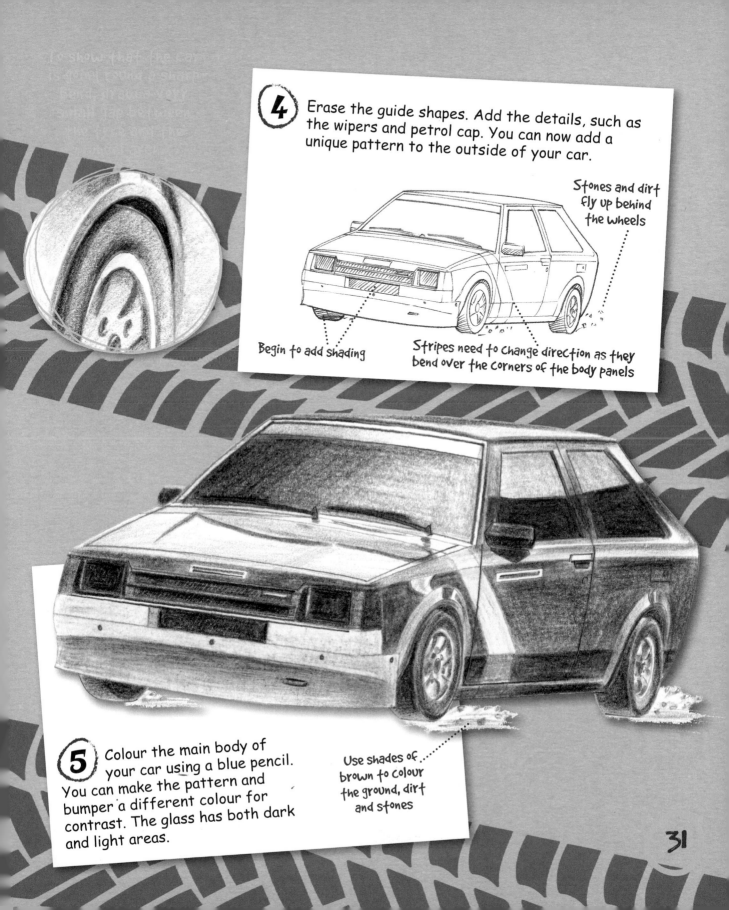

4 Erase the guide shapes. Add the details, such as the wipers and petrol cap. You can now add a unique pattern to the outside of your car.

Stones and dirt fly up behind the wheels

Begin to add shading

Stripes need to change direction as they bend over the corners of the body panels

5 Colour the main body of your car using a blue pencil. You can make the pattern and bumper a different colour for contrast. The glass has both dark and light areas.

Use shades of brown to colour the ground, dirt and stones

Aston Martin

1 Draw a large body box shape. Add a roof box shape with sloping sides on top.

We can see the sloping shape of the back window as the car is viewed from above

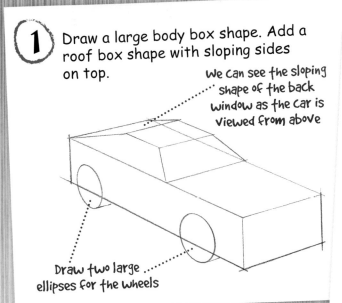

Draw two large ellipses for the wheels

2 Start to shape the front and back of the body of your car. Add shapes for the lights.

Draw a rough shape to form the windows

Start to shape the windscreen with straight lines

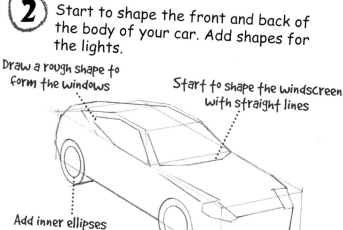

Add inner ellipses to the wheels

3 Make all the corners of the car very smooth and add extra details, such as the radiator grill, number plate and lines of shaping on the bonnet.

The wing mirrors will have straight edges

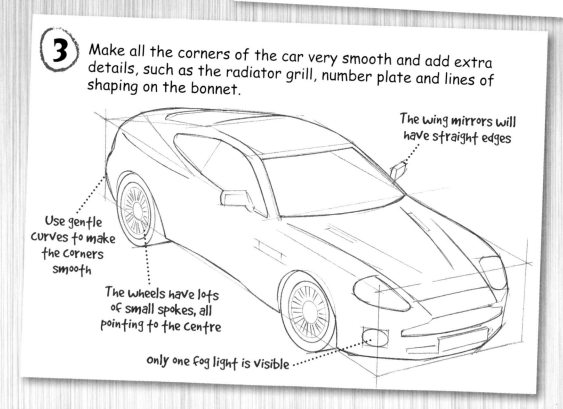

Use gentle curves to make the corners smooth

The wheels have lots of small spokes, all pointing to the centre

only one fog light is visible

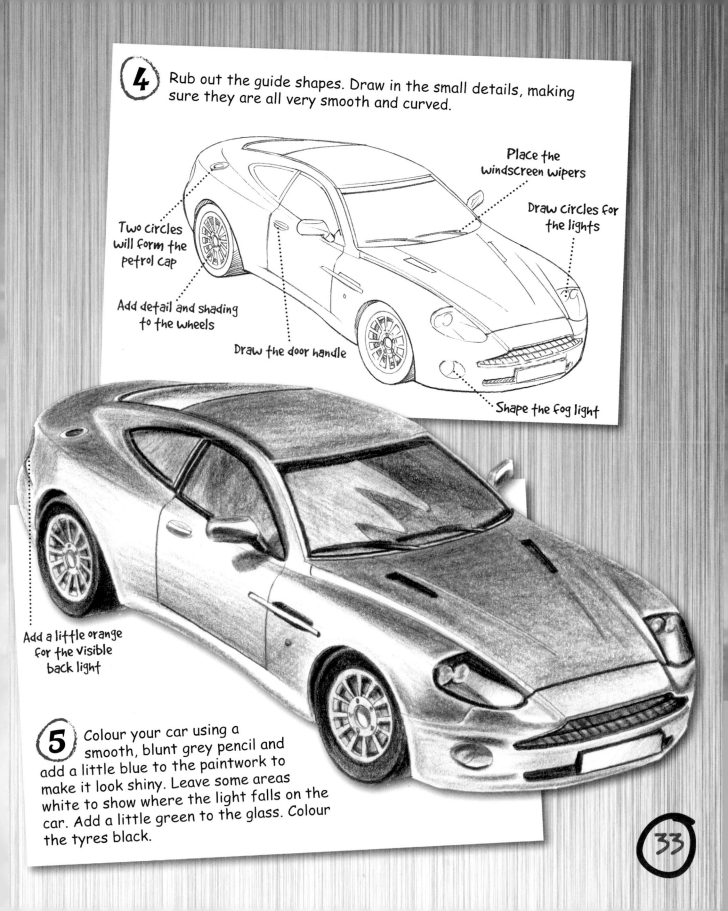

4 Rub out the guide shapes. Draw in the small details, making sure they are all very smooth and curved.

Place the windscreen wipers

Draw circles for the lights

Two circles will form the petrol cap

Add detail and shading to the wheels

Draw the door handle

Shape the fog light

Add a little orange for the visible back light

5 Colour your car using a smooth, blunt grey pencil and add a little blue to the paintwork to make it look shiny. Leave some areas white to show where the light falls on the car. Add a little green to the glass. Colour the tyres black.

Jeep

① Draw a big body box shape for the main part of your car. On top of this add a roof box shape at the back.

The body looks bigger at the front because it is closer

Draw the three visible wheels

Lines will form the front bumper

The back wheel looks smaller and thinner than the front wheels

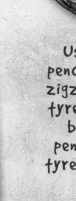

Use a sharp black pencil and draw three zigzag lines to create tyre tread. Use blunt brown and black pencils to shade the tyre around the tread.

② Shape the front of your car. Draw the wheel arches using straight lines.

Start to draw the roof with a peak in the middle

Draw a rectangle for the windscreen

There are no doors — the sides of the car are completely open

Rub out the sections of the wheels hidden by the body

Add inner ellipses to the wheels

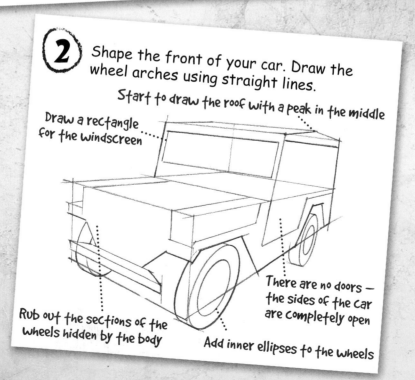

3 Continue to add detail with straight lines. Start to shape the seat inside.

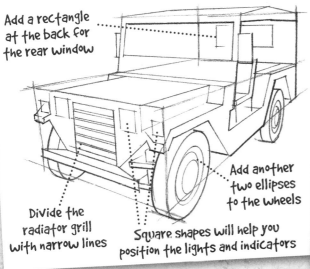

Add a rectangle at the back for the rear window

Divide the radiator grill with narrow lines

Square shapes will help you position the lights and indicators

Add another two ellipses to the wheels

4 Add the details and complete the roof, using curved lines to make it look like it is made of a soft material.

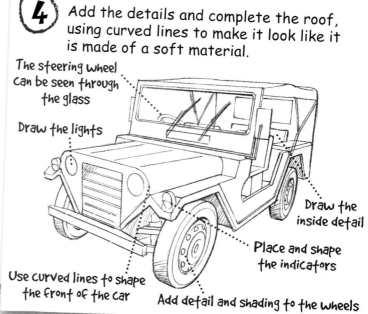

The steering wheel can be seen through the glass

Draw the lights

Use curved lines to shape the front of the car

Place and shape the indicators

Draw the inside detail

Add detail and shading to the wheels

5 Jeeps are often painted in a pattern of green colours for camouflage. Make sure the surfaces are an even colour, as the paint has no shine.

Use an orange pencil to colour the indicators

Ferrari

1 Draw a low, flat body box shape for the main part of the car. On top of this add a small, sloping shape, which will become the windscreen.

The front wheel is a different angle to the back wheel because it is turning

Add the two visible wheels

2 Draw rounded edges at the back and make the front pointed.

Begin to draw the seats

Start to shape the windscreen

Add inner ellipses to the wheels

Shape the long, thin light

Add the radiator grills

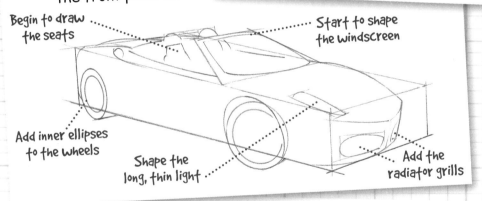

3 Start to make the corners of the car smooth and add extra details. The wheels have five thin, double spokes.

Start to add detail to the lights

Add lines of shaping

The wing mirrors are curved

We can see under the wheel arch, as the wheel is turned

4 Rub out the guide shapes and draw the details. Add shading to the lights, radiator grills and under the wheel arches.

The steering wheel and rearview mirror can be seen through the windscreen

Shade the vent

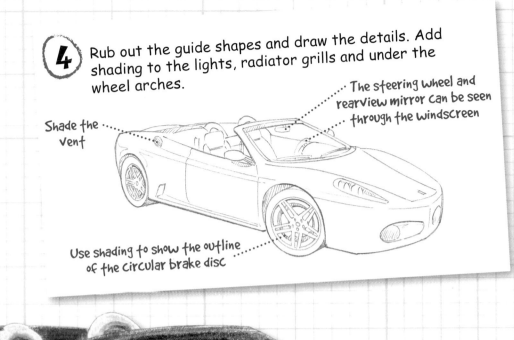

Use shading to show the outline of the circular brake disc

Adding a green tint to the glass will make the yellow seats look slightly green through it

5 Use smooth, even pencil strokes to build up the glossy red paintwork. The leather seats can be coloured in shades of yellow and light brown.

Mercedes

1 Draw a body box shape, much lower at the front than at the back. Add a roof box shape on top, towards the back.

Draw ellipses for the three wheels that will be visible

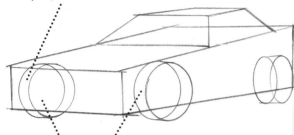

These wheels are slightly turned, so they look wider than the back wheel

2 Draw the outlines of the doors and the door openings using straight lines.

The doors open upwards

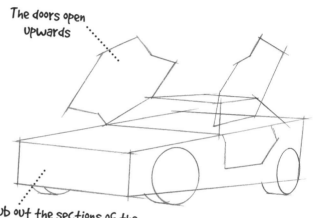

Rub out the sections of the wheels hidden behind the body

3 Begin to shape the body of your car and the doors. Draw the windows in the doors using straight lines.

Add a circular badge

Draw the radiator grill using gentle curves

Draw two ellipses on the wheels

Square shapes will help position the lights

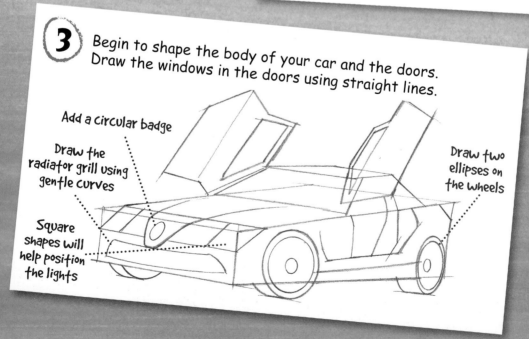

4 Erase the guide shapes and shape the body using curved lines. Add the details.

Draw two circle shapes each side of the front for the lights

Add lines of shaping

The wing mirrors are curved

Add ten gently curved spokes in each wheel

Circles will form the fog lights

Begin to add shading

Lights are made of glass, so use a mix of blue and green colours. Draw lines of black shading that are thick at one end and thin at the other to make it look like there are ridges in the glass.

5 The silver paint is very shiny. Use an orange pencil on the sides to show the reflection of the ground and a blue pencil on top to show the reflection of the sky. Colour the radiator grills and the tyres black and use green in the windows.

Red leather seats are not very shiny, so they need to be an even colour

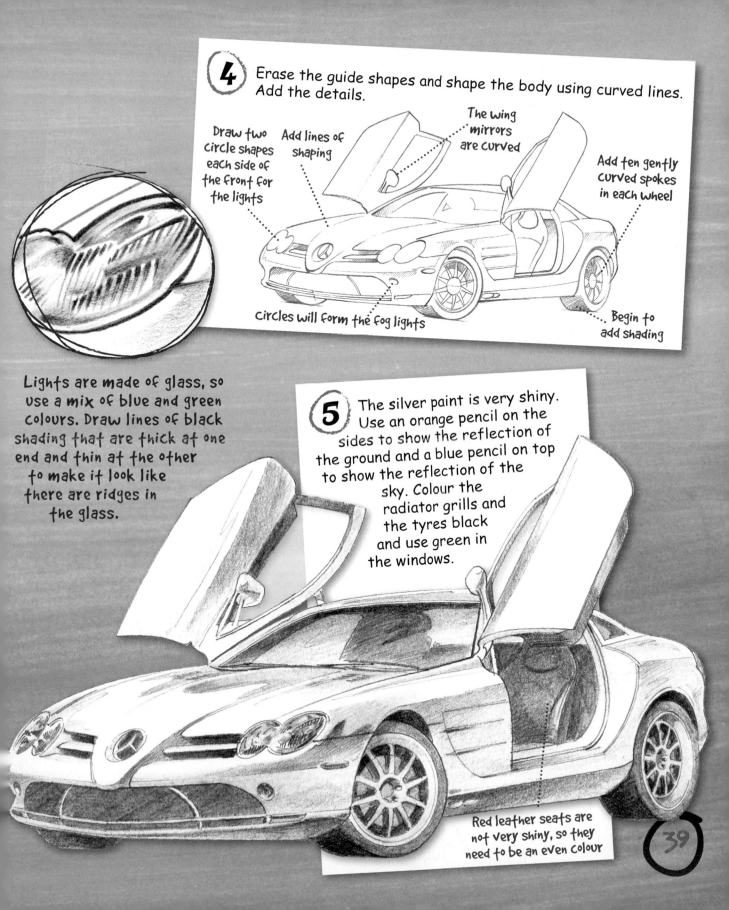

Rally car

1
Draw a sloped body box shape for the main body of the car and a roof box shape on top. Add ellipses for the four wheels, as they will all be visible.

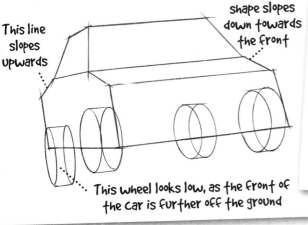

This line slopes upwards

The body box shape slopes down towards the front

This wheel looks low, as the front of the car is further off the ground

2
Add rough shapes for the front lights and the radiator grills.

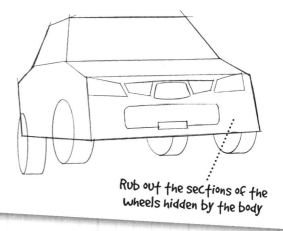

Rub out the sections of the wheels hidden by the body

3
Begin to shape the corners of the body. Add the wheel arches and inner ellipses to the wheels.

Add a shape for the windows

Make the corners rounded

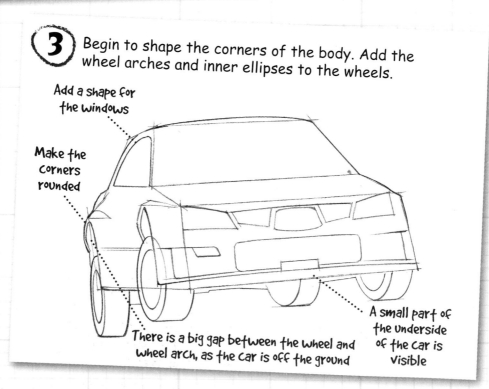

There is a big gap between the wheel and wheel arch, as the car is off the ground

A small part of the underside of the car is visible

4 Add detail to the wheels and add the final bodywork parts, such as the rear spoiler, the door handles and the wing mirrors.

Place the roof vent ·······

Draw unique graphics on your car

Begin to shade under the wheel arches

Draw the spokes and shade the wheels

Add stones and dirt flying up

Shade the radiator grills

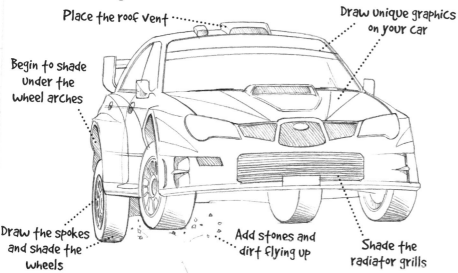

Use sharp brown and orange pencils to draw dirt and stones flying up from the tyres. Draw little lines behind them or smudge them with your finger to make them look like they are flying up.

Gold wheels can be shown with yellow and orange pencils

5 Colour your car red and leave the graphics white for contrast. The underside of the car needs to be dark. Use different shades of blue and green for the glass. Add lines of tread to the tyres.

F1 racing car

1
Draw a shallow body box shape and four huge wheels. On top of the body box shape, add a triangle shape at the back of the car.

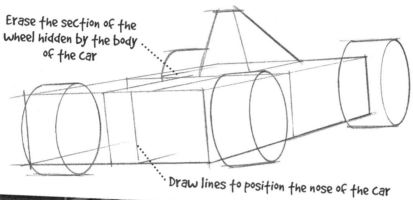

Erase the section of the wheel hidden by the body of the car

Draw lines to position the nose of the car

2
Draw the big spoilers at the front and back of the car. Add inner ellipses to the wheels.

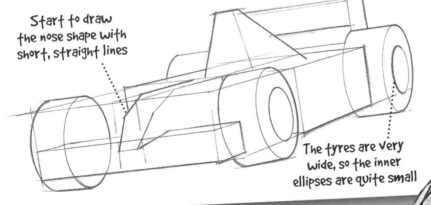

Start to draw the nose shape with short, straight lines

The tyres are very wide, so the inner ellipses are quite small

The detail in the wheels is blurred to show that they are spinning fast. Use a blunt pencil to make the edges of the shapes soft. Then use your finger to gently smudge the colour, making it even softer.

3 Begin to shape the sides of the car and the front spoiler. Add a circle in the centre for the drivers helmet.

Add the small mirrors

Create a gentle curve for the nose shape

Draw straight lines joining the body of the car to the large front wheels

4 Use curved lines to finish shaping the body. Shade the holes in the body and the wheels.

Shade and add a pattern to the driver's helmet

Add extra ellipses to the large wheels

Start to add graphics to your car

5 Colour the car green and the graphics red and white for contrast. The top surfaces should be the lightest. There is no tread on the tyres, so colour them slowly to make sure they look smooth.

Make the tops of the tyres pale, as the light is shining on them

Gallery

HAVE A LOOK AT THESE PAGES FOR EXTRA INSPIRATION. THERE ARE IDEAS FOR LOTS OF DIFFERENT WAYS TO DRAW CARS AND MANY DIFFERENT EFFECTS YOU CAN CREATE.

Different angles

The same car looks different when viewed from different angles. The front of this Aston Martin looks big when it is viewed from the front, but the car looks long when viewed from the side.

Reflections

Clean, shiny cars reflect their surroundings. Metal, glass and gleaming paintwork all reflect light in different ways.

Shadows

Cars cast dark shadows on the ground beneath them. Use a black pencil to add shadows to your pictures.

Movement

When you draw a car moving fast, make the background blurred. You can also blur the car itself by smudging it with your finger. Adding smoke and even flames will make the car's movement look dramatic.

Driving conditions

Have fun drawing cars driving through water, snow or sand. You could even draw a car driving up a rocky slope, instead of on a flat road.

First published as hardback in 2009 by Miles Kelly Publishing Ltd
Harding's Barn, Bardfield End Green, Thaxted, Essex, CM6 3PX, UK

Copyright © Miles Kelly Publishing Ltd 2009

This edition published 2011

2 4 6 8 10 9 7 5 3 1

PUBLISHING DIRECTOR Belinda Gallagher
CREATIVE DIRECTOR Jo Cowan
EDITORIAL DIRECTOR Rosie McGuire
EDITOR Sarah Parkin
DESIGNER Michelle Foster
COVER DESIGNER Kayleigh Allen
REPROGRAPHICS Anthony Cambray, Stephan Davis
REPROGRAPHICS ASSISTANT Charlie Pearson
PRODUCTION MANAGER Elizabeth Collins

ISBN 978-1-84810-492-1

Printed in China

British Library Cataloguing-in-Publication Data
A catalogue record for this book is available from the British Library

ACKNOWLEDGEMENTS
The publishers would like to thank the following sources
for the use of their photographs:
Page 9(l) Wikipediq, Cars en travel, (m) Wikipedia, IFCAR, (r) BMW AG;
10(r) Courtesy of Land Rover, (l) Wikipedia, Ypy31; 11(t) BMW AG,
(br) Wikipedia, Ypy31, (bl) Mercedes-Benz UK; 13(b) BMW AG;
16–17 (background) Kirsty Pargeter/Fotolia.com; 20–21 (background)
Lizard/Fotolia.com; 26–27 (background) Sharpshot/Fotolia.com;
44 Images courtesy of Aston Martin; 45(bl) Mercedes-Benz UK;
47(mr) Courtesy of Land Rover, (bl) BMW AG, (br) Courtesy of Land Rover

All other images are from the Miles Kelly Archives

Additional illustrations by Carl Venton at Maltings Partnership

With thanks to the pupils at St Peter's C of E Primary School,
Coggeshall, for their help with this book

Made with paper from a sustainable forest

www.mileskelly.net
info@mileskelly.net

www.factsforprojects.com

Self-publish your
children's book

buddingpress.co.uk